"If you aren't radical but want to be, or used to be but wore out, *The Radical Bible* is all you need. It may be your last chance. For sure, it's your best chance."

— Colman McCarthy
Washington Post Columnist

"Rich, challenging and contemporary, Kevin Ahern's version of *The Radical Bible* is an old friend renovated substantially to serve us well in these challenging times."

— Marie Dennis
Director, Maryknoll Office for Global Concerns
Co-President, Pax Christi International

About **KEVIN AHERN**

Kevin Ahern is past president of the International Movement of Catholic Students. Founded in 1921, it is headquartered in Paris and brings together more than seventy-five national federations of Catholic university students from six continental regions. A learned and dynamic young Christian, he is a Maryknoll affiliate and has been involved with Catholic NGOs at the UN, and is currently getting his doctorate in theological ethics at Boston College.

THE *Radical* BIBLE

Compiled by
KEVIN AHERN

Maryknoll, New York 10545

Founded in 1970, Orbis Books endeavors to publish works that enlighten the mind, nourish the spirit, and challenge the conscience. The publishing arm of the Maryknoll Fathers and Brothers, Orbis seeks to explore the global dimensions of the Christian faith and mission, to invite dialogue with diverse cultures and religious traditions, and to serve the cause of reconciliation and peace. The books published reflect the views of their authors and do not represent the official position of the Maryknoll Society. To learn more about Maryknoll and Orbis Books, please visit our website at www.maryknollsociety.org.

Copyright © 2009 by Orbis Books.

Published by Orbis Books, Maryknoll, NY 10545-0308.

All rights reserved. No part of this publication may be reproduced or transmitted in any form or by any means, electronic or mechanical, including photocopying, recording, or any information storage or retrieval system, without prior permission in writing from the publisher.

Queries regarding rights and permissions should be addressed to Orbis Books, P.O. Box 308, Maryknoll, NY 10545-0308.

Manufactured in the United States of America.

Library of Congress Cataloging-in-Publication Data

The radical Bible / compiled by Kevin Ahern.
    p. cm.
  Includes bibliographical references.
  ISBN 978-1-57075-816-4 (pbk.)
  1. Christianity – Developing countries. I. Ahern, Kevin.
BR115.U6E34 2009
261.8 – dc22

                                      2008040117

Contents

Introduction: The Bible: A Book of Reflection, Prayer, and Action	7
1. Our Global Reality	13
2. What Is Scripture Saying to Us?	18
3. The World Was Made for Everyone	22
4. Early Israel: Model for Humanity	32
5. God Is on the Side of the Oppressed	53
6. The Kingdom of Peace: A Utopia	70
7. A New Beginning	83
8. New People of God	125
9. A New Creation	147
Suggestions for Action	153
Further Reading	159
Notes	163

INTRODUCTION

The Bible

A Book of Reflection, Prayer, and Action

For many of us, the word "radical" might not be the first thing that comes to mind when we think about the Bible. However, if we look at the meaning of the word, which refers to the *root* or ultimate source, the Bible is very radical — addressing the deepest questions of our existence: our relationship to God, our relationship to others, and our relationship to creation.

Throughout both the Hebrew and Christian Scriptures we see over and over again calls to repentance, conversion, and acts of love and justice. In reflecting on the "roots" of these messages, we can discover, as many saints, prophets and martyrs have before us, a specific spirituality — a spirituality that calls us both to prayerful discernment and to loving action.

In an effort to shed light on this spirituality and to help make it more relevant to our lives today, *The Radical Bible* links a selection of scriptural passages with contemporary social issues facing our world as highlighted by the commentaries of prophetic witnesses of social justice.

As many of these social witnesses affirm, the Bible is not meant to be a passive or dead text to be read and studied like any other book. As the Word of God, it is meant to be a living text where we can discover and come closer to God through prayerful reflection on the text, reflection in community, social analysis, and action in the world. In the Gospel of Matthew, Jesus points to this by teaching that those who act upon his words are like those who build their house on rock, while those who do not respond are like those who build their house on sand. In the end, only those who build their house on a solid foundation will be able to survive the storm (Matt. 7:24–27).

The Radical Bible is intended to be a tool for personal and group reflection for those seeking to respond to God's radical call to reflection and action in the world. By its very nature this project is selective, and it does not seek to be a comprehensive overview of Scripture or the thoughts of the prophets selected. Recognizing that Scripture does not offer clear solutions to the multifaceted problems facing our world, we have selected passages from the Bible that speak to the root messages of human dignity, creation, solidarity, justice, discipleship, and love. It is hoped that those reading this text will be inspired to look more in depth at the Bible, the context of the selections, biblical commentaries, and the full writings of spiritual witnesses such as the ones presented alongside the scriptural quotations. It is hoped that by reflecting on the root messages of the Bible that people of faith can become more attentive to the many diverse prophetic voices in our communities and in our world.

At the end of the book, you will find a list of references and suggestions for further reading. Many of the selected quotations come from the Modern Spiritual Masters Series of Orbis Books.

INTRODUCTION

The *Radical Bible* is an updated version of the 1972 adaptation by John Eagleson and Philip Scharper of the *bibel provokativ* (1969) by Hellmut Haug and Jürgen Rump. This present version keeps many of the scriptural selections presented in the previous edition, while adding a new set of contemporary social commentaries that respond more directly to our present global reality.

All scriptural quotations are used with permission from the *Christian Community Bible: Catholic Pastoral Edition*, published by Claretian Publications, Philippines (2005).

Thank you to all those who helped in the renewal of this project, especially to Michael Leach and Doris Goodnough at Orbis Books and to my supportive family and friends.

ONE

Our Global Reality

> One-fifth of humanity live in countries where many people think nothing of spending $2 a day on a cappuccino. Another fifth of humanity survive on less than $1 a day and live in countries where children die for want of a simple anti-mosquito bed net.
>
> —UN *Human Development Report,* 2005[1]

We live in a world marked by gross inequalities and injustices, a world where:

- 40 percent of the world's population, 2.6 billion people, live in *poverty* — struggling to survive on less than two dollars a day.

- 33 million people live with *HIV/AIDS*, a disease that claimed the lives of 2 million women, men, and children in 2007.

- Every year over a million people die of *malaria*, mostly children.

- Approximately 10 million *children* die before the age of five, the vast majority from preventable causes resulting from poverty, malnutrition, and a lack of access to basic health care.

- *Global warming*, a result of human activity, continues to have a devastating impact on our environment. Massive deforestation, carbon emissions, and pollution are having a visible impact on our ecosystem — often negatively impacting the lives of the poor who are most vulnerable to the "natural" environmental disasters.

- As many as 700,000 women, men, and children are *trafficked* each year, often for sexual slavery or forced labor.
- More than half a million women die annually in *childbirth*.
- Dozens of *wars and violent conflicts* kill and displace millions. The Iraq War alone has resulted in the death and forced migration of millions of innocent civilians.
- As a result of conflict, poverty, and environmental disasters, there are presently more than 8 million *refugees* and as many as 23.7 million internally displaced persons.
- The GDP (gross domestic product) of the Heavily Indebted Poor Countries

(567 million people) is less than the combined wealth of the world's seven richest individuals.

—UN *Human Development Report*, 2007/2008;
Coalition of Catholic Organizations
Against Human Trafficking[2]

Reality in the Wealthiest Nation on Earth

- 36.5 million people, including 12.8 million children, live below the *poverty* line in the United States.
- 47 million Americans, or 16 percent of the population, were *without health insurance* in 2005.
- The 2007 U.S. *military budget* (not including Iraq and Afghanistan) is over 439 billion U.S. dollars, larger than

that of the next 168 biggest military spenders combined.

- Economist Joseph Stiglitz has recently estimated the total *cost of the wars in Iraq and Afghanistan* will be more than 3 trillion U.S. dollars.

—Catholic Campaign for Human Development;
U.S. Department of Defense[3]

TWO

What Is Scripture Saying to Us?

How are people of faith and good will to respond to the reality of our world? What can be done in the face of such complex and overwhelming challenges and injustices?

As many prophets of our time have testified, the Word of God, as a living book, calls us to respond to these challenges with a radical biblical spirituality, which is both mystical and prophetic.

This spirituality calls for an integral or holistic faith, which seeks to overcome the false dichotomy between faith and life and which recognizes the communal

WHAT IS SCRIPTURE SAYING TO US?

dimension of biblical faith. This is well summarized in the *Kairos Document,* a statement issued by Christian leaders in the midst of the South African apartheid system:

The Bible does not separate the human person from the world in which he or she lives; it does not separate the individual from the social or one's private life from one's public life. God redeems the whole person as part of his whole creation (Rom. 8:18–24). A truly biblical spirituality would penetrate into every aspect of human existence and would exclude nothing from God's redemptive will. Biblical faith is prophetically relevant to everything that happens in the world.[4]

With such an integral spirituality, we cannot sit idly by in the face of injustices in the world. Our faith in the God of history, as St. James reminds us, must be expressed in concrete action in our world:

What good is it, my brothers and sisters, to profess faith without showing works? Such faith has no power to save you. If a brother or sister is in need of clothes or food and one of you says, "May things go well for you; be warm and satisfied," without attending to their material needs, what good is that? So it is for faith without deeds: it is totally dead.... So just as the body is dead without its spirit, so faith without deeds is also dead.

—James 2:14–17, 26

As many of the contemporary prophets of justice remind us, such action in the world can be meaningful and effective only if it is grounded in contemplation and prayerful discernment (Rom. 12:2), which will allow us to see and respond to the root causes of the injustices in our world. To understand how to develop and deepen an integral spirituality of action, it may be helpful to start at the beginning — the book of Genesis.

THREE

The World Was Made for Everyone

The book of Genesis deals with some of the most fundamental and radical questions of human existence: why and how we were made; how we are to relate to God; how we are to relate to others; and how we are to relate to God's precious and good gift of creation.

Genesis presents to us the truth of the dignity and sacredness of human life. We can discover that all of us, female and male, were created in the image and likeness of God, a belief that stands at the root of our present conceptions of human rights. We also discover that in addition to our "rights," we have specific responsibilities toward God's gift of creation and to the other members of the human family (Am I my brother's keeper?).

- *In your own lives, how do you reflect and respond to these truths of creation?*

In the Image and Likeness of God

God said, "Let us make man in our image, to our likeness...." So God created man in his image; in the image of God he created him; male and female he created them. God blessed them and said to them "Be fruitful and increase in number, fill the earth and subdue it, rule over the fish of the sea and the birds of the sky, over every living creature that moves on the ground."... God saw all that he had made and it was very good.

—Genesis 1:26–28, 31

Around us, life bursts forth with miracles—
a glass of water, a ray of sunshine, a leaf,
a caterpillar, a flower, laughter, raindrops.
If you live in awareness, it is easy to see
miracles everywhere. Each human being is a
multiplicity of miracles everywhere. Eyes that
see thousands of colors, shapes, and forms;
ears that hear a bee flying or a thunderclap;
a brain that ponders a speck of dust as easily
as the entire cosmos; a heart that beats in
rhythm with the heartbeat of all beings. When
we are tired and feel discouraged by life's
daily struggles, we may not notice these
miracles, but they are always there.

—Thich Nhat Hanh[5]

THE WORLD WAS MADE FOR EVERYONE

To choose life involves rejecting every form of violence: the violence of poverty and hunger which afflicts so many human beings; the violence of armed conflict; the violence of criminal trafficking in drugs and arms; the violence of mindless damage to the natural environment. In every circumstance, the right to life must be promoted and safeguarded with appropriate legal and political guarantees, for no offence against the right to life, against the dignity of any single person is ever unimportant. —Pope John Paul II[6]

Nuclear war *threatens* life on a previously unimaginable scale; abortion *takes* life daily on a horrendous scale; public executions are fast becoming weekly events in the most advanced technological society in history; and euthanasia is now openly discussed and even advocated. Each of these assaults on life has its own meaning and morality; they cannot be collapsed into one problem, but they must be confronted as pieces of a larger pattern.... No one is called to do everything, but each of us can do something. —Cardinal Joseph Bernardin[7]

Gift of Creation

God said, "I have given you every seed-bearing plant which is on the face of all the earth, and every tree that bears fruit with seed. It will be for your food. To every wild animal, to every bird of the sky, to everything that creeps along the ground, to everything that has the breath of life, I give every green plant for food." So it was. —Genesis 1:29–30

Care for the earth and for the environment is a moral issue. Protecting the land, water, and

THE WORLD WAS MADE FOR EVERYONE — 27

air we share is a religious duty of stewardship and reflects our responsibility to born and unborn children, who are most vulnerable to environmental assault. Effective initiatives are required for energy conservation and the development of alternate, renewable, and clean-energy resources. —U.S. Catholic Bishops[8]

In today's world, it is the poor who are bearing the brunt of climate change. Tomorrow, it will be humanity as a whole that faces the risks that come with global warming. The rapid build-up of greenhouse gases in the Earth's atmosphere is fundamentally changing the climate forecast for future generations. We are edging toward "tipping points." These are unpredictable and non-linear events that could open the door to ecological catastrophes — accelerated collapse of the Earth's great ice sheets being a case in point — that will transform patterns of human settlement and undermine the viability of national economies. Our generation may not live to see the consequences. But our children and their grandchildren will have no alternative but to live with them. Aversion to poverty and inequality today, and to catastrophic risk in the future provides a strong rationale for urgent action.

—UN *Human Development Report,* 2007/2008[9]

Humanity, if it truly desires peace, must be increasingly conscious of the links between natural ecology, or respect for nature, and human ecology. Experience shows that disregard for the environment always harms human coexistence, and vice versa. It becomes more and more evident that there is an inseparable link between peace with creation and peace among men. Both of these presuppose peace with God. —Pope Benedict XVI[10]

Responsibilities toward Others

Yahweh said to Cain, "Where is your brother, Abel?" He answered, "I don't know; am I my brother's keeper?" Yahweh asked, "What have you done? Your brother's blood cries out to me from the ground." —Genesis 4:9–10

We recognize that, as members of one human family, we are called to build a world based on true solidarity, which makes it impossible for us to sit idly by while others are suffering. We therefore recognize that we cannot separate our rights from our responsibilities to protect and respect the rights of others.

—*Charter of Catholic Student Rights and Responsibilities*[11]

Ubuntu is very difficult to render into a Western language. It speaks of the very essence of being human.... It is to say, "My humanity is caught up, is inextricably bound up, in yours." We belong in a bundle of life. We say, "A person is a person through other persons." It is not, "I think therefore I am." It says rather: "I am human because I belong. I participate, I share." A person with *ubuntu* is open and available to others, affirming of others, does not feel threatened that others are able and good, for he or she has a proper self-assurance that comes from knowing that he or she belongs in a greater whole and is diminished when others are humiliated or diminished, when others are tortured or oppressed, or treated as if they were less than who they are.

—Archbishop Desmond Tutu[12]

We stand at a critical moment in Earth's history, a time when humanity must choose its future. As the world becomes increasingly interdependent and fragile, the future at once

THE WORLD WAS MADE FOR EVERYONE

holds great peril and great promise. To move forward we must recognize that in the midst of a magnificent diversity of cultures and life forms we are one human family and one Earth community with a common destiny.

We must join together to bring forth a sustainable global society founded on respect for nature, universal human rights, economic justice, and a culture of peace. Toward this end, it is imperative that we, the peoples of Earth, declare our responsibility to one another, to the greater community of life, and to future generations. —Preamble of the *Earth Charter*[13]

FOUR

Early Israel

Model for Humanity

After Genesis, the following four books of the Bible tell how a group of foreign workers in Egypt, led by Moses, is chosen by God for a special relationship — a covenant. As a part of this new relationship, God led the people out of their experience of oppression, revealed to them the Law, and brought them to the Promised Land. In exchange, God's people accepted the Law and from it they organized a society and a kingdom.

As we can see in the books of the Law, biblical Israel from its very beginning was to be something very different. It was not meant to be like its oppressive neighboring kingdom of Egypt, because it was the kingdom of God's chosen people. As such, it was to be guided by the virtues of justice, love, and solidarity which were revealed to them by God. Central to this vision, as highlighted by the call of the jubilee, was the importance of establishing right relationships with oneself, one's neighbor, and God.

For God's chosen people, all dimensions of life — social, business, and personal — were to be lived differently. Relationships and social structures were to give special attention to those most marginalized from society, especially the orphans, the widows, and the foreigners.

- *How does the experience of oppression and injustice shape how one experiences God?*

- *How does our faith enter into our personal and business relationships?*
- *Do the present social structures of our world take into account the needs of the marginalized?*

Deliverance from Oppression

Yahweh said, "I have seen the humiliation of my people in Egypt and I hear their cry when they are cruelly treated by their taskmasters. I know their suffering. I have come down to free them from the power of the Egyptians and to bring them up from that land to a beautiful spacious land, a land flowing with milk and honey.

"Go now! I am sending you to Pharaoh to bring my people, the sons of Israel, out of Egypt." —Exodus 3:7–10

EARLY ISRAEL: MODEL FOR HUMANITY

Throughout the Bible, God appears as the liberator of the oppressed. He is not neutral. He does not attempt to reconcile Moses and Pharaoh, to reconcile the Hebrew slaves with their Egyptian oppressors or to reconcile the Jewish people with any of their late oppressors. Oppression is sin and it cannot be compromised with; it must be done away with. God takes sides with the oppressed.

—*Kairos Document*[14]

No, it is not God's will that a few rich people enjoy the goods of this world and exploit the poor. No, it is not God's will that some people remain poor and abject forever. No, religion is not the opiate of the people; it is a force that exalts the lowly and casts down the proud, that feeds the hungry and sends the sated away empty.

—Letter of the Peoples of the Third World[15]

Called to Solidarity

When you reap the harvest of your land do not reap the extreme limits of your field or gather the gleanings after your harvest. Do not strip your vineyard bare and do not gather the grapes that have fallen; leave them for the needy and the stranger. I am Yahweh, your God.

Do not steal or lie or deceive one another....

Do not oppress your neighbor or rob him. The wages of a hired man are not to remain with you all night until morning. You shall not curse a deaf man nor put a stumbling block in the way of the blind; but you shall fear your God; I am Yahweh....

Do not seek revenge or nurture a grudge against one of your people, but love your neighbor as yourself; I am Yahweh. —Leviticus 19:9–18

The burden of being black and the burden of being white is so heavy that it is rare in our society to experience oneself as a human being. It may be, I do not know, that to experience oneself as a human being is one with experiencing one's fellows as human beings. Precisely what does it mean to experience oneself as a human being? In the first place, it means that the individual must have a sense of kinship to life that transcends and goes beyond the immediate kinship of family or the organic kinship that binds him ethnically or "racially" or nationally. He has to feel that he belongs to his total environment. He has a sense of being an essential part of the structural relationship that exists between him and all other men, and between him, all other men, and the total external environment. As a human being, then, he belongs to life and the whole kingdom of life that includes all that lives and perhaps, also, all that has ever lived. In other words, he sees himself as part of a continuing, breathing, living existence. To be a human being, then, is to be essentially alive in a living world. —Howard Thurman[16]

[Solidarity] is not a feeling of vague compassion or shallow distress at the misfortunes of so many people, both near and far. On the contrary, it is a firm and persevering determination to commit oneself to the common good; that is to say, to the good of all and of each individual, because we are all really responsible for all. —Pope John Paul II[17]

Solidarity points toward the neuralgic issue of U.S. politics: taxation. Taxes are one way in which the state facilitates our responsibilities to each other. Tax policy is a secular issue,

EARLY ISRAEL: MODEL FOR HUMANITY   39

but it is rooted in moral obligations we have to one another. A fair tax policy, one which obliges each of us to play a role in sustaining the human dignity of all in our society, is a requirement of distributive justice. In Catholic teaching, paying taxes is a virtue. Taxes help us to meet our pre-existing obligations to the poor.   —Cardinal Joseph Bernardin[18]

You Must Remember Egypt

Do not exploit the lowly and the poor daily-wage earner, whether he be one of your brothers or a foreigner whom you find in your land....

Do not violate the right of the foreigner, or of the orphan, or take as pledge the clothing of a widow. Remember that you were a slave in Egypt and Yahweh, your

God, rescued you. This is why I command you to do this.

When you harvest the wheat in your fields, if you drop a sheaf, do not return to pick it up, but let it be there for the foreigner, the orphan and the widow. Yahweh will bless you for this in all your work. —Deuteronomy 24:14, 17–19

In the modern world, where there are still grave inequalities between rich countries and poor countries, and where advances in communications quickly reduce distances, the immigration of people looking for a better life is on the increase. These people come from less privileged areas of the earth and their arrival in developed countries is often perceived as a threat.... Institutions in host countries must keep careful watch to prevent the spread of the temptation to exploit foreign laborers, denying them the same rights enjoyed by

EARLY ISRAEL: MODEL FOR HUMANITY — 41

nationals, rights that are to be guaranteed to all without discrimination.

— *Compendium of the Social Doctrine of the Church*[19]

At times one hears that the present globalized world offers new possibilities of life to poor peoples, especially by means of migration. There is no need to exclude that possibility, nor to deny that migration may alleviate some evils, especially when it happens out of dire necessity. However, the migrations today are not a simple readjustment of the human species — something that has occurred often in history and can be potentially enriching. Present-day migrations, because of their causes and the ways they take place, are especially cruel. —Jon Sobrino, S.J.[20]

The Gospel mandate to "welcome the stranger" requires Catholics to care for and stand with immigrants, both documented and undocumented, including immigrant children. Comprehensive reform is urgently necessary to fix a broken immigration system and should include a temporary work program with worker protections and a path to permanent residency; family reunification policies; a broad and fair legalization program; access to legal protections, including due process and essential public programs; refuge for those fleeing persecution and exploitation; and policies to address the root causes of migration. —U.S. Catholic Bishops[21]

The Promise of the Jubilee

When seven Sabbaths of years have passed, that is seven times seven years, there shall be the time of the seven weeks of the years, that is forty-nine years. Then on the tenth day of the seventh month

sound the trumpet loudly. On this Day of Atonement sound the trumpet all through the land. Keep holy the fiftieth year and proclaim freedom for all the inhabitants of the land. It shall be a jubilation year for you when each one shall recover his property and go back to his family.
—Leviticus 25:8–10

Today all developing countries in the world ... have huge debts to repay. They owe money to private companies, usually international banks; to governments; and to international institutions like the World Bank and the International Monetary Fund. By the end of 2004, external debt of Sub-Saharan countries stood at US$231 billion. At the same time, the Gross Domestic Product of these countries was just about US$350 billion. In other words, African countries cannot pay back their debts and sustain development. Most countries have to spend more than 20 percent of their revenues to service the debt.... Debt becomes an ethical issue when it poses a major obstacle to the full enjoyment of human rights. In as far as debt servicing reduces people to poverty while its creditors determine Kenya's political, economic, and social destiny, then debt is essentially a human rights issue and a moral concern for a Christian.

—Catholic Bishops of Kenya[22]

Trade Justice

If you lend money to any of my people who are poor, do not act like a moneylender and do not charge him interest. If ever you take a person's cloak as a pledge, you must give it back to him by sunset, for it is all the covering he has for his body. In what else will he sleep? And when he cries to me I will hear him, for I am full of pity. —Exodus 22:24–25

If your brother becomes poor and is unable to support himself, help him. Help this stranger or this guest that he may live with you. Do not take interest from him, but fear your God, so that your brother may live among you. Do not give him your silver at interest nor your food for gain. —Leviticus 25:35–37

The World Bank and IMF [International Monetary Fund] support the OECD [Organisation for Economic Co-operation and Development] goal of poverty reduction, but they refuse to accept poverty eradication as an issue of justice and human rights. Whenever a powerful multilateral lending institution begins a solidarity discourse, churches must put some critical distance so as to be able to read between the lines. It is not gratuitous that the ones who hold the money bag suddenly express their concern for the poor, especially when the poor are struggling to enjoy life regardless of oppression and injustice. The struggle for justice and peace that is so close to the heart of the Gospel of God's reign demands that life cannot be reduced to an economic growth that, as experience demonstrates, only benefits the powerful. —World Council of Churches[23]

The cultural ideal of the Western industrialized world is the self-made, self-sufficient, autonomous individual who stands by himself or herself, not needing anyone else (except for sex) and not beholden to anyone for anything.... From the point of view of all other cultures in the world, past and present, this is simply unintelligible. In other cultures, the person who is separated and isolated from the rest of the community would be regarded

EARLY ISRAEL: MODEL FOR HUMANITY — 47

as very unfortunate. Interdependence, social coherence, and reliance upon one another are highly appreciated cultural values. In Africa we say: "A person becomes a person through other people." In other words, your identity depends upon the family, the friends, and the community who relate to you and to whom you relate.... Western individualism is spreading throughout the world. It is part of neo-liberal globalization and it is destroying other more communitarian cultures in its wake.

—Albert Nolan, O.P.[24]

We have remained so impressed by the success of the free market that we never dared to express any doubt about our basic assumption.... I support globalization and believe it can bring more benefits to the poor than its alternative. But it must be the right kind of globalization. To me, globalization is like a hundred-lane highway criss-crossing the world. If it is a free-for-all highway, its lanes will be taken over by the giant trucks from powerful economies. Bangladeshi rickshaws will be thrown off the highway. In order to have a win-win globalization we must have traffic rules, traffic police, and traffic authority for this global highway. The rule of "strongest takes it all" must be replaced by rules that ensure that the poorest have a place and piece of the action, without being elbowed out by the strong. Globalization must not become financial imperialism. —Muhammad Yunus[25]

Justice for the Poor

Do not take from the poor man just because he is poor or condemn the one in misfortune, because Yahweh will intercede for them. —Proverbs 22:22

> *Give justice to the weak and the orphan; defend the poor and the oppressed. Rescue the helpless and the needy; deliver them from the hand of the wicked.*
>
> —Psalm 82:3–4

In reality, the link between faith and justice is much more intrinsic and radical than any universal ethical obligation. The Scriptures, in addition to recognizing universal ethical obligations, also question the ability of any moralism, even a politically correct moralism, to effectively change the world. From the biblical viewpoint, the relationship between faith and justice constitutes a Gospel, a piece of good news, which irrupts into a world of oppression and opens up a way of justice which that world by itself could barely imagine.

—Antonio Gonzalez[26]

I refuse to accept the idea that man is mere flotsam and jetsam in the river of life which surrounds him. I refuse to accept the view that mankind is so tragically bound to the starless midnight of racism and war that the bright daybreak of peace and brotherhood can never become a reality.... I believe that wounded justice, lying prostrate on the blood-flowing streets of our nations, can be lifted from the dust of shame to reign supreme among the children of men.... When our days become dreary with low-hovering clouds and our nights become darker than a thousand midnights, we will know that we are living in the creative turmoil of a genuine civilization struggling to be born.

—Dr. Martin Luther King, Jr.[27]

Go Tell It on the Mountain

Speak on behalf of the dumb and defend the cause of all those who are destitute. Open your mouth, pronounce just sentences, defend the needy and the poor.
— Proverbs 30:8–9

Climate change demands urgent action now to address a threat to two constituencies with little or no political voice: the world's poor and future generations. It raises profoundly important questions about social justice, equity, and human rights across countries and generations.
— UN *Human Development Report,* 2007/2008[28]

Each time we look upon the poor, on the farm workers who harvest the coffee, the sugarcane, or the cotton or the farmer who joins the caravan of workers looking to earn their savings for the year...remember, there is the face of Christ.... The face of Christ is among the sacks and baskets of the farmworkers; the face of Christ is among those who are tortured and mistreated in the prisons; the face of Christ is dying of hunger in the children who have nothing to eat; the face of Christ is in the poor who ask the church for their voice to be heard. How can the church deny this request when it is Christ who is telling us to speak for him?

—Archbishop Oscar Romero[29]

FIVE

God Is on the Side of the Oppressed

Not too long after God's deliverance from the oppression of Egypt and the establishment of Israel, life began to get difficult again for God's chosen people.

Imbalances of power and wealth, greed and external aggressions seemed to be tearing apart the community, which would never again be the same. A schism divided the community into two conflicting kingdoms, Judah and Israel. Many Israelites were adopting other religious customs, and the neighboring Assyrian and Chaldean forces invaded and occupied the Promised Land.

In the context of these political and social realities, the Holy Spirit inspired prophetic voices to call the Israelites and all those in positions of power and wealth to change their ways and act justly, especially toward the marginalized groups in society. These prophets warned of God's judgment if things did not change and if the injustices and oppressions continued. In our world today, marked by such extreme poverty and extreme wealth, we hear new cries for justice, peace, and solidarity.

- *What do the words of the prophets say to the injustices and power imbalances of our world today?*

- *Who are the prophetic voices of our world today? What are they saying to us?*

Woe to Those Who Ignore the Poor

Woe to those proud people who live overconfident on the hill.... You lie on beds inlaid with ivory and sprawl on your couches; you eat lamb from the flock and veal from calves fattened in the stall.... You drink wine by the bowlful and anoint yourselves with the finest oils, but you do not grieve over the ruins of Joseph.

—Amos 6:1, 4, 6

My experience tells me that the kingdom of God is within us, and that we can realize it not by saying "Lord, Lord," but by doing God's will and God's work. If therefore we wait for the kingdom to come as something coming from outside, we shall be sadly mistaken. Do you know that there are thousands of villages where people are starving and which are on the brink of ruin? If we would listen to the voice of God, I assure you we would hear God say that we are taking God's name in vain if we do not think of the poor and help them. If you cannot render the help that they need, it is no use talking of service of God and service of the poor. —Mohandas Gandhi[30]

The poor person is the one who has been converted to God and puts all his faith in him, and the rich person is one who has not been converted to God and puts his confidence in idols: money, power, material things.... Our works should be directed toward converting ourselves and all people to this authentic meaning of poverty. —Archbishop Oscar Romero[31]

You Have Devoured the Vineyard

Yahweh takes his place in court and stands to try his people. Yahweh calls

> *to judgment the elders and the princes: "You have devoured my vineyard. The spoils of the poor is in your houses. What right have you to crush the people and to grind down the poor?" declares Yahweh Sabaoth.*
> —Isaiah 3:13–15

> The globalization that many people are protesting about today is the globalization of a particular economic culture, neo-liberal capitalism, a thoroughly materialistic worldview based on the principle of the survival of the fittest, a culture that destroys other cultures and indigenous wisdom, making the rich richer and the poor poorer around the world.
> —Albert Nolan, O.P.[32]

No one today is unaware of this divide between the world's rich and poor. No one today can claim ignorance of the cost that this divide imposes on the poor and dispossessed who are no less deserving of human dignity, fundamental freedoms, security, food, and education than any of us. The cost, however, is not borne by them alone. Ultimately, it is borne by all of us—North and South, rich and poor, men and women of all races and religions.

Today's real borders are not between nations, but between powerful and powerless, free and fettered, privileged and humiliated. Today, no walls can separate humanitarian or human rights crises in one part of the world from national security crises in another.

—Kofi Annan[33]

You Have Trampled upon the Poor

Woe to those who plot wickedness and plan evil even on their beds! —Micah 2:1

GOD IS ON THE SIDE OF THE OPPRESSED

Hear this, you who trample on the needy to do away with the weak of the land. You who say, "When will the new moon or the sabbath feast be over so that we may open the store and sell our grain? Let us lower the measure and raise the price; let us cheat and tamper with the scales, and even sell the refuse with the whole grain. We will buy up the poor for money and the needy for a pair of sandals." Yahweh, the pride of Jacob, has sworn by himself, "I shall never forget their deeds."

—Amos 8:4–7

In the last thirty years, trafficking of women and children in Asia for sexual exploitation alone has victimized more than 30 million people. Children are trafficked for a number of purposes, including sexual exploitation, child labor, participation in armed conflict, adoption and marriage. Globally, the main trafficking routes are from south to north and east to west. The CIA estimates that fifty thousand people are trafficked into the United States each year. The victims of trafficking or their caregivers usually seek to escape from poverty. Some children are enticed by promises of education or a good job. Others are kidnapped outright, seized from their homes and then bought and sold like commodities.

—Helene O'Sullivan, M.M.[34]

Your Rich Are Full of Violence

The voice of Yahweh calls to the city, in order to save those who fear his Name. "Is there still within you unjust wealth and accursed short measure? Shall I approve your false scales and your bags of false weights? O city whose rich are full of violence, whose citizens speak falsehood, people of deceitful tongue! See, I am striking you a grievous blow, making you desolate because of your sins. You shall eat but not be satisfied." —Micah 6:9–14

The population of the affluent world is nourished on a steady diet of brutal mythology and hallucination, kept at a constant pitch of high tension by a life that is intrinsically violent in that it forced a large part of the population to submit to an existence which is humanly intolerable.... The problem of violence, then, is not the problem of a few rioters and rebels, but the problem of a whole structure which is outwardly ordered and respectable, and inwardly ridden by psychopathic obsessions and delusions. —Thomas Merton[35]

To satisfy the demands of justice and equity, strenuous efforts must be made, without disregarding the rights of persons or the natural qualities of each country, to remove as quickly as possible the immense economic inequalities, which now exist and in many cases are growing and which are connected with individual and social discrimination.

—Second Vatican Council[36]

Nobel economist Dr. Joseph Stiglitz calculates that the war in Iraq, if it continues another eight years, will ultimately cost the U.S. economy 2.2 trillion dollars. It's shocking to think of what we've lost in dedicating this expenditure to war, rather than to domestic and foreign aid which could save millions of lives lost to hunger and illness, or, say, to renewable energy development which might save hundreds of millions from economic and environmental disasters now clearly on the horizon. Who are the criminals?   —Kathy Kelly[37]

The Masses Will Awaken

Woe to him who amasses what is not his and fills himself with extorted pledges. Your creditors will come suddenly, your money collectors will waken and take away all of your goods. Since you have plundered so many nations, shedding blood, stripping the land, their cities and homes, all the remaining nations will turn on you. —Habakkuk 2:6–8

Some of those who call me a subversive, a Communist, a red, must do so in jest or in malice. But there are others who really believe it and who pray for my conversion. I inquired once about the basis for that absurd accusation. A general explained it to me thus: "When you set out to convert the masses into persons, Bishop, you say that literacy isn't enough, that you want to conscientize them—to open their eyes, make them look at the facts, awaken their initiative, teach them to work together and not wait till city hall acts for them. But don't you see you are unleashing a force that tomorrow you won't be able to control? It is a lot easier to conscientize than to carry out structural reforms. That's why, if you keep on conscientizing the masses, you are a subversive. And since you are setting one class against the other, you are a Communist—or at least doing their work."

The answer to the general seems obvious to me. With us, without us, or perhaps despite us, the masses are going to wake up.

—Dom Helder Camara[38]

Let Justice Prevail

Seek good and shun evil, that you may live. Then Yahweh, the God of hosts, as you have claimed, will be with you.

GOD IS ON THE SIDE OF THE OPPRESSED — 65

Hate wickedness and love virtue and let justice prevail. —Amos 5:14–15

You have been told...what is good and what Yahweh requires of you: to do justice, to love mercy, and to walk humbly with your God. —Micah 6:8

The Gospel is primarily a message of salvation. The construction of the world is a task for human beings on this earth. To state the question of a theology of liberation means, therefore, to ask about the meaning of this work on earth, the work that human beings perform in this world vis-à-vis the faith.... The theology of liberation means establishing the relationship that exists between human emancipation—in the social, political, and economic orders—and the kingdom of God.

—Gustavo Gutiérrez[39]

Because we are individual and social beings, our actions for justice must be both personal and political. What we do, how we live, and what we consume are all personal justice issues. Our working lives are what we spend the bulk of our time on and so we are called to choose work that builds a more just world.... If our work is ultimately in opposition to justice and love, then we must find other work. Likewise, our family lives must reflect the values of Micah. But despite the challenges of incorporating justice and love into our personal lives, there is more, much more.

...Unfortunately, we start from a peculiarly uncomfortable global social justice position. We North Americans sit comfortably at the very top of the world economic mountain. Over 3 billion of our sisters and brothers live beneath us on $2 a day. They are subjected to needless and manmade economic, political, religious, and military injustices, many of which directly support our position atop the mountain. Because of this, we have a responsibility to help transform the unjust structures and institutions that create or contribute to their suffering. We must support those who are working for justice locally and globally. We must join with others in social justice movements that are working to challenge these global practices of injustice. We must also help create new simpler ways of living that are not built on the foundations of injustice. —Bill Quigley[40]

Sacred Space or Den of Thieves

These words were spoken by Yahweh to Jeremiah, "Stand at the gate of Yahweh's house and proclaim this in a loud voice: ... It is far better for you to amend your ways and act justly with all. Do not abuse the stranger, orphan, or widow or shed innocent blood in this place or follow false gods to your own ruin.... But you trust in deceptive and useless words. You steal, kill, take the wife of your neighbor; you swear falsely, worship Baal, and follow foreign gods who are not yours. Then, after doing all these horrible things you come and stand before me in this temple that bears my Name and say, 'Now we are safe.'

Is this house on which rests my Name a den of thieves?" —Jeremiah 7:1–11

We all know that Christ has, in effect, been eliminated from our lives. Of course, we build him a temple, but we live in our own houses. Christ has become a matter of the church of, rather, of churchiness of a group, not a matter of life.... However, one thing is clear: we understand Christ only if we commit ourselves to him in a stark "Either-Or." He did not go to the cross to ornament and embellish our life. If we wish to have him, then he demands the right to say something decisive about our entire life. —Dietrich Bonhoeffer[41]

SIX

The Kingdom of Peace

A Utopia

As part of their prophetic calls for a new way of living, a community structured on solidarity and justice, the prophets envisioned the coming of a new order, a utopic kingdom brought about by a just and peaceful leader, a messiah.

In this call, the prophets do not excuse us from our role in helping to bring about this new just and peaceful order, because the new ruler will judge us by our actions, especially in how we treat the poor.

For many in our world today, there is a feeling that the problems we face

THE KINGDOM OF PEACE: A UTOPIA

are too big and too complex to change so why even bother. Such a situation of hopelessness or complacency is not helped by the fact that it is in the interests of those in positions of political, military, media, and economic power to maintain the status quo. In looking to the coming of the prince of peace and to new heavens and a new earth, the prophets help us to have hope as the World Social Forum movement echoes that *another world is possible* and that even our smallest actions, like the mustard seed (Matt. 13:31–32) can have a big impact.

- *What are the elements that we imagine when we think about a new just and peaceful world?*

- How do we help to work toward that kingdom in our daily lives?

Swords into Plowshares

In the last days, the mountain of Yahweh's house shall be set over the highest mountains and shall tower over the hills.

All the nations shall stream to it, saying "Come let us go to the mountain of the Lord, to the house of the God of Jacob, that he may teach us his ways and we may walk in his paths."

He will rule over the nations and settle disputes for many peoples. They will beat their swords into plowshares and their spears into pruning hooks. Nation will not raise sword against nation; they will train for war no more.

THE KINGDOM OF PEACE: A UTOPIA

O nation of Jacob, come, let us walk in the light of the Lord! —Isaiah 2:1–5

Today countries are concentrating too much on efforts and means to defend their borders. Yet these countries know so little about the poverty and suffering that make the human beings who live inside such borders feel so lonely! If instead they would worry about giving these defenseless beings some food, some shelter, some health care, some clothes, it is undeniable that the world would be a more peaceful and happy place to live.

—Mother Teresa[42]

Violence rests on the assumption that the enemy and I are entirely different: the enemy is evil, and I am good. The enemy must be destroyed, but I must be saved. But love sees things differently. It sees that even the enemy suffers from the same sorrows and limitations that I do. That we both have the same hopes, the same needs, the same aspiration for peaceful and harmonious human life. And that death is the same for both of us. Then love may perhaps show me that my brother is not really my enemy and that war is both his enemy and mine. War is *our* enemy. Then peace becomes possible. —Thomas Merton[43]

The Just and Peaceful Leader

O God, endow the king with your justice, the royal son with your righteousness. May he rule your people justly and defend the rights of the lowly. Let the mountains bring peace to the people, and the hills justice. He will defend the cause of the poor, deliver the children of the needy, and crush the oppressor.... All the kings bow down to him, and all nations serve him.

THE KINGDOM OF PEACE: A UTOPIA

He delivers the needy who call on him, the afflicted with no one to help them. His mercy is upon the weak and the poor; he saves the life of the poor. He rescues them from oppression and strife, for this life is precious to him.... May his name endure forever. —Psalm 72:1–4, 11–14, 17

Moral leadership requires a vision of peace and justice for the entire human family. This vision goes beyond our national borders to see the benefits of global peace and justice for ourselves and all people. Visionary leaders lift that vision up for all to see and then point the way forward to make that vision of peace a reality here and now. If we had authentic, moral leaders, everyone would be inspired to join the great work at hand — the task of abolishing hunger, poverty, homelessness, the death penalty, war, and nuclear weapons.

—John Dear, S.J.[44]

The world lacks neither the financial resources nor the technological capabilities to act. If we fail to prevent climate change it will be because we were unable to foster the political will to cooperate. Such an outcome would represent not just a failure of political imagination and leadership, but a moral failure on a scale unparalleled in history.

—UN *Human Development Report,* 2007/2008[45]

A New World

I now create new heavens and a new earth, and the former things will not be remembered, nor will they come to mind again.... The sound of the weeping will not be heard in it any more. You will no longer know of dead children or of adults who do not live out a lifetime.... They

THE KINGDOM OF PEACE: A UTOPIA

will build houses and dwell in them; they will plant crops and eat their fruit. No longer will they build houses for others to dwell in; no longer will they plant for others to eat....

The wolf and the lamb will feed together, the lion will eat straw like the ox. They will not destroy or do harm over all my holy mountain.

—Isaiah 65:17–22, 25

A more just world will likely be a more peaceful world, a world less vulnerable to terrorism and other violence. The United States has the responsibility to take the lead in addressing the scandal of poverty and underdevelopment. Our nation should help to humanize globalization, addressing its negative consequences and spreading its benefits, especially among the world's poor. The United States also has a unique opportunity to use its power in partnership with others to build a more just and peaceful world.... It should provide political and financial support for beneficial United Nations programs and reforms, for other international bodies, and for international law, so that together these institutions may become more responsible and responsive agents for addressing global problems.

—U.S. Catholic Bishops[46]

Today we are faced with a challenge that calls for a shift in our thinking, so that humanity stops threatening its life-support system. We are called to assist the Earth to heal her wounds and in the process heal our own—indeed, to embrace the whole creation in all its diversity, beauty, and wonder. This will happen if we see the need to revive our sense of belonging to a larger family of life, with which we have shared our evolutionary process.

THE KINGDOM OF PEACE: A UTOPIA

> In the course of history, there comes a time when humanity is called to shift to a new level of consciousness, to reach a higher moral ground. A time when we have to shed our fear and give hope to each other. That time is now.
> —Wangari Maathai[47]

The Prince of Peace

From the stump of Jesse a shoot will come forth; from his roots a branch will grow and bear fruit. The Spirit of the Lord will rest upon him — a Spirit of wisdom and understanding, a Spirit of counsel and power, a Spirit of knowledge and fear of the Lord. Not by appearance will he judge, nor by what is said must he decide, but with justice he will judge the poor and with righteousness decide for the meek.

Like a rod, his word will strike the oppressor and the breath of his lips slay the wicked. Justice will be the girdle of his waist, truth the girdle of his loins.

The wolf will dwell with the lamb, the leopard will rest beside the kid, the calf and the lion cub will feed together and a little child will lead them. Befriending each other, the cow and the bear will see the young ones lie down together. Like cattle, the lion will eat hay. By the cobra's den, the infant will play. The child will put his hand into the viper's lair.

No one will harm or destroy over my holy mountain, for as water fills the sea the earth will be filled with the knowledge of the Lord. —Isaiah 11:1–9

The present war crisis is something we have made entirely for and by ourselves. There is in reality not the slightest logical reason for war, and yet the whole world is plunging headlong into frightful destruction, and doing so *with the purpose of avoiding war and preserving peace!* This is a true war-madness, an illness of the mind and the spirit.... Of all the countries that are sick, America is perhaps the most grievously afflicted. —Thomas Merton[48]

The United States spends more on the military than any other country.... Where is this money coming from?... As people of faith, we are called to alleviate suffering and end injustice. That work must include addressing a militarism that robs the poor of one country to bomb the poor of another.

We need steps that will lead to a durable, affordable peace and stability. We need to more broadly define security beyond borders, militaries, and hardware; to use all the tools in our toolbox; to dismantle the enduring influence of the military-industrial complex; to commit to use force only as a last resort; and to recalibrate our priorities so that health care, infrastructure, and education are allocated adequate resources.

—Frida Berrigan[49]

SEVEN

A New Beginning

Like the prophets before him, Jesus of Nazareth called those in positions of political, economic, and religious power to task for their abuses, hypocrisy, and especially for their mistreatment of the marginalized. But Jesus was much more than a prophet. As the Son of Man, the Word of God made flesh, Jesus was the prince of peace, the messiah, the one foretold by the prophets. Instead of re-establishing a new earthly kingdom of Israel, as many hoped for, Jesus rejects the temptations to political, economic, and military power and announces the kingdom of God, a kingdom of justice, compassion, and radical love — thus establishing something very new.

In the Gospels we see the signs of this new beginning not only in Jesus' words, but also in his actions, in his embrace and love of the outcast, the marginalized, and the sinners. God's deep love for all of us is reflected in his life, which culminated in being put to death on a cross by the civil powers, and in his resurrection.

In the Gospels we discover God's challenge to discipleship. A challenge to embrace the message of Christ in our hearts, our minds, and our actions — a challenge to work for the construction of a new world, a world of liberation, love, compassion, solidarity, and justice. The fact that this goal may seem impossible or unrealistic should not stop us from answering the call of Christ, for nothing is impossible with God.

A NEW BEGINNING

- *What does the good news of the Gospel say to us in a world of injustice, suffering, and violence?*
- *What do the teachings of Jesus say to our conceptions of power, wealth, and security?*

Prepare the Way of the Lord

John proclaimed a baptism for repentant people to obtain forgiveness of sins, and he went through the whole county bordering the Jordan River. It was just as is written in the book of the prophet Isaiah: listen to this voice crying out in the desert: prepare the way of the Lord, make his path straight. The valleys will be filled and the mountains and hills made low. Everything crooked will be made straight and the rough paths smooth; and every mortal will see the salvation of God.

The people asked him, "What are we to do?" And John answered, "If you have two coats, give one to the person who has none, and if you have food, do the same."
—Luke 3:3–6, 10–11

Repentance means more than just being sorry. It means both admitting that the course you have been on is wrong and committing to begin walking in a new direction. ...Repentance has to do with transformation, and that's exactly what the American church needs to break out of its conformity to the American government's foreign policy of fear and war. There is a better way. The global church feels it, and the world is hungry for it....

Nationalism doesn't go well with the kingdom of God. The church is the international

A NEW BEGINNING

Body of Christ, and "God Bless America" is not found in the Bible. To take a global perspective on politics, to value other countries' interests as much as our own, and, perhaps most critically, to count all the world's children as important as our own—all will significantly alter our political views.

—Jim Wallis[50]

After having been baptized by John the Baptist in the Jordan River, Jesus went into the wilderness and stayed there for forty days in order to strengthen the Holy Sprit in himself. During those forty days he must have sat and walked, practicing walking meditation and sitting meditation. Unfortunately, the Gospels did not record the way he sat and the way he walked. But Jesus did sit and walk.

—Thich Nhat Hanh[51]

The Handmaid of the Lord

And Mary said: "My soul proclaims the greatness of the Lord, my spirit exults in God my savior! He had looked upon his servant in her lowliness and people forever will call me blessed. The Mighty One has done great things for me, Holy is his Name! From age to age his mercy extends to those who live in his presence. He has acted with power and done wonders, and scattered the proud with their plans. He has put down the mighty from their thrones and lifted up those who are downtrodden. He has filled the hungry with good things but has sent the rich away empty." —Luke 1:46–54

Most dramatically, far from being a pious plaster saint, Mary speaks radical, political words about the revolutionary deeds God has

A NEW BEGINNING 89

done for justice and peace.... Just as Mary became a prophet of nonviolence, so too we are called to become prophets of nonviolence and justice. We have to publicly denounce war and injustice, announce God's reign of peace and justice, and point out God's active nonviolence in history. True humility, as Mary shows, means being a servant of the God of peace, and speaking God's word of peace, even to a culture addicted to violence and war.

—John Dear, S.J.[52]

The Beginning of a Ministry

When Jesus came to Nazareth where he had been brought up, he entered the synagogue on the Sabbath as he usually did. He stood up to read and they handed him the book of the prophet Isaiah.

> *Jesus then unrolled the scroll and found the place where it is written: "The Spirit of the Lord is upon me. He has anointed me to bring good news to the poor, to proclaim liberty to the captives and new sight to the blind; to free the oppressed and announce the Lord's year of mercy."*
>
> *Jesus then rolled up the scroll, gave it to the attendant, and sat down, while the eyes of all in the synagogue were fixed on him. Then he said to them, "Today these prophetic words come true even as you listen."*
>
> —Luke 4:16–21

One essential dimension of the life and ministry of Jesus was his commitment to creating a just and inclusive community. He deliberately moved to the margins to embrace the excluded. He evaluated social structures in first-century Palestine from the perspective of the excluded. And he acted

A NEW BEGINNING

to change the structures — structures that *applied* the Roman occupation, structures that *sustained* the privileges of the Judean ruling class, structures that excluded the lepers, the women, the others called "unclean" — with such dedication that it got him killed. His vision was of an inclusive community. He set out to make it real, and he invited us, *called* us, to follow him.

—Marie Dennis[53]

The sign of the coming of the messiah is the suppression of oppression: the messiah arrives when injustice is overcome. When we struggle for a just world in which there is no servitude, oppression, or slavery, we are signifying the coming of the messiah. Therefore the messianic promises bind tightly together the kingdom of God and better living conditions for human beings or, as Paul VI said, more humane living conditions. An intimate relationship exists between the kingdom and the elimination of poverty and misery. The kingdom comes to suppress injustice.

—Gustavo Gutiérrez[54]

Jesus Sides with the Poor

Then looking at his disciples, Jesus said, "Fortunate are you who are poor, the kingdom of God is yours. Fortunate are you who are hungry now, for you will be filled. Fortunate are you who weep now, for you will laugh. Fortunate are you when people hate you, when they reject you and insult you and number you among criminals, because of the Son of Man. Rejoice in that day and leap for joy, for a great reward is kept for you in heaven."
—Luke 6:20–23

A NEW BEGINNING

As followers of Christ, we are challenged to make a fundamental "option for the poor" — to speak for the voiceless, to defend the defenseless, to assess lifestyles, policies, and social institutions in terms of their impact on the poor. This "option for the poor" does not mean pitting one group against another, but rather, strengthening the whole community by assisting those who are the most vulnerable. As Christians, we are called to respond to the needs of all our brothers and sisters, but those with the greatest needs require the greatest response.　　　　　　　—U.S. Catholic Bishops[55]

The essence of being a Christian is to live and act in sympathy with God's Spirit as Jesus did. This implies that we have to be known for keeping the company of beggars, thieves, prostitutes, tax collectors in whatever names and forms that they come to us today. When we take option in favor of the poor we must know that poor people are not a random cross-section of population because poverty does not come randomly. You are more likely to be poor if you are of lower caste, indigenous, black, woman, or under eighteen years of age. Poor people lack opportunities to realize their potential. They lack power, influence, voice, and they are extremely vulnerable to sickness, violence, and disasters. —Musimbi Kanyoro[56]

Blessed Are You

When Jesus saw the crowds, he went up the mountain. He sat down and his disciples gathered around him. Then he spoke and began to teach them:

Fortunate are those who are poor in spirit, for theirs is the kingdom of heaven. Fortunate are those who mourn, they shall be comforted. Fortunate are the gentle, they shall possess the land. Fortunate are those who hunger and thirst for justice, for they shall be satisfied. Fortunate are the merciful, for they shall find mercy. Fortunate are those with a pure heart, for they shall see God.

Fortunate are those who work for peace, they shall be called children of God.

Fortunate are those who are persecuted for the cause of justice, for theirs is the kingdom of heaven.

Fortunate are you, when people insult you and persecute you and speak all kinds of evil against you because you are my followers. Be glad and joyful, for a great reward is kept for you in God.

—Matthew 5:1–12

Jesus' Sermon on the Mount lays out a moral framework for vocational decisions.... By his powerful preaching and by his own life, he emphasized over and over again the privileged place of impoverished and excluded peoples; the great need for compassion and social comforting; the centrality to the discipleship journey of the work for social justice or righteousness; and the call to peacemaking and reconciliation.

To be poor in spirit we have to believe in the equal dignity of every person in the eyes of God and act accordingly. If what we have, where we live, how we spend, or don't spend, our time keeps us from having friends who are poor, then we need to rethink what we have, where we live, and how we spend our time.

To be poor in spirit we have to "live simply so that others may simply live" (Gandhi).... To be poor in spirit we have to live the virtue of solidarity, accompany the poor — next door and on the other side of the world — and interpret reality from their perspective.... To be poor in spirit we have to work with those who are poor to change the structures and transform the systems that create or perpetuate poverty. We have to evaluate laws and public policy proposals and business practices by what they do *to* people who are poor, what they do *for* people who are poor, and what they *enable* poor people to do for themselves.

—Marie Dennis[57]

A New Law of Justice

Then the teachers of Law and the Pharisees brought in a woman who had been caught in the act of adultery. They made her stand in front of everyone. "Master," they said, "this woman has been caught in the act of adultery. Now the Law of Moses orders that such women be stoned to death; but you, what do you say?"

They said this to test Jesus, in order to have some charge against him.

Jesus bent down and started writing on the ground with his finger. And as they continued to ask him, he straightened up and said to them, "Let anyone among you who has no sin be the first to throw a stone at her." And he bent down again, writing on the ground.

As a result of these words, they went away, one by one, starting with the elders, and Jesus was left alone with the woman standing before him. Then Jesus stood up and said to her, "Woman, where are they? Has no one condemned you?" She replied "No one." And Jesus said, "Neither do I condemn you; go away and don't sin again."
—John 8:3–11

I believe Christ is our Truth and is with us always. We may stretch toward it, falling short,

failing seventy times seven, but forgiveness is always there. He is a kind and loving judge.
—Dorothy Day[58]

To walk into a U.S. prison, especially death row, is to enter a desperate world of stern guards, strict regulation, and humiliating body searches.... Society has many misconceptions about prisoners, especially those under a death sentence: that they are incorrigible, irredeemable, brutal, selfish, and uncaring monsters. But in my contacts with condemned men, I have found the contrary. They are poor, spiritually and materially. They know what they have done; all have admitted it. They are sorry for their mistakes and are trying to make restitution in the only way open to them: suffering the misery of incarceration and loss of freedom. All are grateful to whatever kindness is shown to them. They are hungry for love, acceptance, respect, and compassion.

They try to remain human. The idea of the state killing a healthy human being is appalling.

—Marie Nassaur, M.M.[59]

Who Is My Neighbor?

Then a teacher of the Law came and began putting Jesus to the test. And he said, "Master, what shall I do to receive eternal life?" Jesus replied, "What is written in the Scripture? How do you understand it?" The man answered, "It is written: You shall love the Lord God with all your heart, with all your soul, with all your strength and with all your mind. And you shall love your neighbor as yourself." Jesus replied, "What a good answer! Do this and you shall live." The man wanted to keep up appearances, so he replied, "Who is my neighbor?"

Jesus then said, "There was a man going down from Jerusalem to Jericho and he fell into the hands of robbers. They stripped him, beat him, and went off leaving him half-dead.

"It happened that a priest was going along that road and saw the man but passed by on the other side. Likewise a Levite saw the man and passed by on the other side. But a Samaritan, too, was going that way, and when he came upon the man, he was moved with compassion. He went over to him and treated his wounds with oil and wine and wrapped them with bandages. Then he put him on his own mount and brought him to an inn where he took care of him."... Jesus then asked, "Which of these three, do you think, made himself neighbor to the man who fell into the hands of robbers?" The teacher of the Law answered, *"The one*

who had mercy on him." And Jesus said, "Go then and do the same."
—Luke 10, 25–34, 36–37

The Word of God has a religious mission...and a human mission: to love our neighbor means to be concerned about their needs, their concrete situation, and, like the Good Samaritan, to help the poor fallen by the roadside.

—Archbishop Oscar Romero[60]

There is no great difference in reality between one country and another, because it is always people you meet everywhere. They may look different or be dressed differently, they may have a different education or position, but they are all the same. They are all people to be loved; they are all hungry for love.

—Mother Teresa[61]

A NEW BEGINNING

Crumbs from the Table

Once there was a rich man who dressed in purple and fine linen and feasted every day. At his gate lay Lazarus, a poor man covered with sores, who longed to eat just the scraps falling from the rich man's table. Even dogs used to come and lick his sores. It happened that the poor man died and angels carried him to take his place with Abraham. The rich man also died and was buried. From hell where he was in torment, he looked up and saw Abraham afar off, and with him Lazarus at rest.

He called out: "Father Abraham, have pity on me and send Lazarus with the tip of his finger dipped in water to cool my tongue, for I suffer so much in this fire."

Abraham replied: "My son, remember that in your lifetime you were well off while the lot of Lazarus was misfortune."
—Luke 16:19–25

There is no need for an extensive description of poverty in Latin America and the world. It is a world of "Lazaruses."...1.3 billion human beings must live on less than a dollar a day, which is a grave evil for the human species. In theological language this is the "macroblasphemy" of our time.... Those "Lazaruses" coexist with "rich men."... The three best-paid soccer players in the world — an Englishman, a Frenchman, and a Brazilian, who all play on the same Spanish team — earn US$42 million a year; by comparison the San Salvador metropolitan area, with 1,821,532 inhabitants, has an annual budget of $45.6 million. This is comparative harm, a shameless insult to the poor, a failure of the

A NEW BEGINNING

human family. In theological language it is the failure of God in creation. —Jon Sobrino, S.J.[62]

In our attempt to understand and present in its proper light the issue of debt cancellation, we need to turn to the Word of God.... The rich man can be easily seen as representing the North, while poor Lazarus the underdeveloped South. The rich man ignores Lazarus's plight. For this attitude of his, his name has not been recorded while all know the name of the poor man: Lazarus. Ignoring the situation of other people or worse, not caring about what our actions may cause in other people's lives, leads to loss of true human identity: our names will not be remembered. The efforts at debt cancellation that were made till now could be compared to the scraps that Lazarus hoped he could feed on at the foot of the rich man's table: they are illusory promises without real substance. Lazarus still died of hunger and disease! —Catholic Bishops of Kenya[63]

This is the commitment of being a Christian: to follow Christ in his incarnation. If Christ, the God of majesty, became a lowly human and lived with the poor and even died on a cross like a slave, our Christian faith should also be lived in the same way. The Christian who does not want to live this commitment of solidarity with the poor is not worthy to be called Christian. —Archbishop Oscar Romero[64]

Life Is So Much More Than Possessions

Then Jesus said to the people. "Be on your guard and avoid every kind of greed, for even though you have many possessions, it is not that which gives you life."

A NEW BEGINNING

And Jesus continued with this story, "There was a rich man, and his land had produced a good harvest. He thought: 'What shall I do?...I will pull down my barns and build bigger ones to store all this grain, which is my wealth. This I may say to myself: My friend, you have a lot of good things put by for many years. Rest, eat, drink, and enjoy yourself.' But God said to him: 'You fool! This very night your life will be taken from you; tell me who shall get all you have put aside? This is the lot of the one who stores up riches instead of amassing for God.'"

Then Jesus said to his disciples, "I tell you not to worry about your life: What are we to wear? Or about your body: What are we to eat? For life is more than food and the body more than clothing."

—Luke 12:15–23

We are living in an era of consumerism, because this is what is at the very heart of our societies....Consumer goods are necessary and have many advantages, but these advantages should be made universal. We could distribute everything in such a way that everybody could make use of consumer goods. Instead we say that other people can't use cars because they pollute the atmosphere, while we carry on using ours....

Socially responsible consumerism should answer questions like: Do I know what I'm buying? Why am I buying it? What is the social reality behind each one of the products I'm buying? In reality, things can be very different.... The coffee we drink every morning is linked to a very difficult social reality. At this moment, 25 million families (around 125 million people), are living in absolute poverty, because in the last five years the price they receive for each kilo of coffee has gone down by 75 percent; in other words, for each kilo of coffee they receive less than it cost them to produce it. —Adela Cortina and Ignasi Carreras[65]

If we don't pray, we remain attached to earthly things, we become small like them, narrow like them, we get pressured by them, we sell ourselves to them—because we give our love and our heart to them. We must pray!

—Karl Rahner, S.J.[66]

Who Is Your True Master?

It was then that a young man approached him and asked, "Master, what good work must I do to receive eternal life?" Jesus answered, "...If you want to enter eternal life, keep the commandments...."

The young man said to him, "I have kept all these commandments. What is still lacking?" Jesus answered, "If you wish to be perfect, go and sell all you possess and give that money to the poor and you will become the owner of a treasure in heaven. Then come back and follow me."

On hearing this answer, the young man went away sad for he was a man of great wealth.

Then Jesus said to his disciples, "Truly I say to you: it will be hard for one who is rich to enter the kingdom of heaven. Yes, believe me: it is easier for a camel to go through the eye of a needle than for the one who is rich to enter the kingdom of heaven." —Matthew 19:16–17, 20–24

No one can serve two masters; for he will either hate one and love the other, or he will be loyal to the first and look down on the second. You cannot at the same time serve God and money. —Matthew 6:24

A NEW BEGINNING

This term "kingdom of God" appears 112 times in the Gospels, 90 of them attributed to Jesus. His kingdom means that the plan of God for humankind is to be fulfilled in a radically profound way, here on earth. It is a reversal of the usual conditions of society.... Jesus proposed a completely radical change in the value systems. He disapproved of those who did not care for the hungry, naked, homeless, and imprisoned. His followers have to be concerned with justice, sharing, and love rather than with the values of amassing wealth or seeking power and prestige. One cannot serve God and mammon.

—Tissa Balasuriya, O.M.I.[67]

That only a few should care about the poor clearly was not the message of the Sermon on the Mount, but to live in solidarity with those who are poor, to be poor in spirit with all that vocation implies remained a tremendous challenge for followers of Jesus who, like the rich young man in the Gospel have "many possessions" or already busy lives (Mark 10:23). —Marie Dennis[68]

The Last Judgment

"When the Son of Man comes in his glory with all his angels, he will sit on the throne of his glory. All the nations will be brought before him, and as a shepherd separates the sheep from the goats, so will he do with them, placing the sheep on his right and the goats on his left.

"The King will say to those on his right: 'Come, blessed of my Father! Take possession of the kingdom prepared for you from the beginning of the world. For I was hungry and you fed me, I was thirsty and you gave me drink. I was a

A NEW BEGINNING

stranger and you welcomed me into your house. I was naked and you clothed me. I was sick and you visited me. I was in prison and you came to see me.'

"*Then the good people will ask him: 'Lord, when did we see you hungry and give you food; thirsty and give you drink, or a stranger and welcome you, or naked and clothe you? When did we see you sick or in prison and go to see you?' The King will answer, 'Truly, I say to you: whenever you did this to these little ones who are my brothers and sisters, you did it to me.'*

"*Then he will say to those on his left: 'Go cursed people, out of my sight into the eternal fire which has been prepared for the devil and his angels! For I was hungry and you did not give me anything to eat, I was thirsty and you gave me nothing to drink; I was a stranger and you did not welcome me.... Truly I say*

to you whatever you did not do for one of these little ones, you did not do for me.'"
—Matthew 25:31–45

The day will come when nations will be judged not by their military or economic strength, or by the splendor of their capital cities and public buildings, but by the well-being of their peoples: by their levels of health, nutrition, and education; by their opportunities to earn a fair reward for their labors; by their ability to participate in the decisions that affect their lives; by the respect that is shown for their civil and political liberties; by the provision that is made for those who are vulnerable and disadvantaged; and by the protection that is afforded to the growing minds and bodies of their children. —UNICEF[69]

Love Is the Way

"You have heard that it was said: An eye for an eye and a tooth for a tooth. But I tell you this: do not oppose evil with evil; if someone slaps you on your right cheek, turn and offer the other. If someone sues you in court for your shirt, give your coat as well. If someone forces you to go one mile, go also the second mile. Give when asked and do not turn your back on anyone who wants to borrow from you.

"You have heard that it was said: Love your neighbor and do not do good to you enemy. But this I tell you: Love your enemies, and pray for those who persecute you, so that you may be children of your Father in Heaven. For he makes his sun rise on both the wicked and the good."

— Matthew 5:43–45

There is nothing that we can do but love, and dear God — please enlarge our hearts to love each other, to love our neighbor, to love our enemy as well as our friend.... We are supposed to love as Christ loved, to the extent of laying down our lives for our brothers. That was the New Commandment.... To accept the least place, to sit back, to ask nothing for ourselves, to serve each other, to lay down our lives for our brothers, this is the strange upside-down teaching of the Gospel.... We have not yet begun to learn about love. Now is the time to begin, to start afresh, to use this divine weapon.

—Dorothy Day[70]

The Power of Prayer

When you pray, do not use a lot of words. ... Your Father knows what you need, even before you ask him.

A NEW BEGINNING

This, then, is how you should pray: Our Father in heaven, holy be your name, your kingdom come and your will be done, on earth as it is in heaven.

Give us this day our daily bread. Forgive us our debts just as we forgive those who are in debt to us. Do not bring us to the test but deliver us from the evil one.

If you forgive others their wrongs, your Father in heaven will also forgive yours.
—Matthew 6:7–14

Our service of God and of the church does not consist only in talking and doing. It can also consist in periods of silence, listening, waiting. Perhaps it is very important in our era of violence and unrest to rediscover meditation, silent inner unitive prayer, and creative Christian silence. —Thomas Merton[71]

Action without meditation, without prayer and a spiritual life, is suicide for our faith and love. If you are supposed to bring Jesus to others, how much you must live in him, love him, and be close to him. —Mother Teresa[72]

Prayer is not an old woman's idle amusement. Properly understood and applied, it is the most potent instrument of action. Let us then pray and find out what we have meant by nonviolence and how we shall retain the freedom gained by its use. —Mohandas Gandhi[73]

Broken for You

When Jesus had finished washing their feet, he put on his garment again, went back to the table, and said to them, "Do you understand what I have done to you?

A NEW BEGINNING

...I have given you an example that as I have done, you also may do."
—John 13:12, 15

While they were eating, Jesus took bread, said a blessing and broke it, and gave it to his disciples saying, "Take and eat; this is my body." Then he took a cup and gave thanks and passed it to them saying, "Drink this, all of you, for this is my blood, the blood of the Covenant, which is poured out for many for the forgiveness of sins." —Matthew 26:26–28

In the Eucharist, we worship the God of nonviolence, encounter the nonviolent Jesus, and become people of nonviolence.... Jesus' last Passover meal is intimately connected to his first commandment to love one another and to love our enemies, and his last commandment, to put down our swords. Jesus lived, taught and practiced nonviolence, and he wants us to do the same. —John Dear, S.J.[74]

The Mass is the spiritual food that sustains me. I could not pass a single day or hour in my life without it. In the Eucharist, I see Christ in the appearance of bread. In the slums, I see Christ in the distressing disguise of the poor—in the broken bodies, in the children, in the dying.
—Mother Teresa[75]

Today, however, all of us, Protestant and Catholics, need that tangible, physical act of participating in the body and blood of the crucified and risen Christ. The sacrament of communion is the most profound religious expression of the virtue of solidarity, as Pope John Paul II defines it.... It is in that moment that we become members one of another that we not only partake of the Eucharist but can actually become Eucharist. —Robert Bellah[76]

Jesus comes to me every morning in Holy Communion: I repay him in my very small way by visiting the poor. —Blessed Pier Giorgio Frassati[77]

The Way of the Cross

The Roman soldiers took Jesus into the palace of the governor and the whole troop gathered around him and dressed him in a purple military cloak. Then, twisting a crown of thorns, they forced it onto his head, and placed a reed in his right hand. They knelt before Jesus and mocked him.... They spat on him, took the reed from his hand, and struck him on the head with it.

When they had finished mocking him, they pulled off the purple cloak and dressed him in his own clothes again, and led him out to be crucified.... There they crucified him and divided his clothes among themselves. —Matthew 27:27–31, 35

If our Christianity has ceased to be serious about discipleship, if we have watered down the Gospel into emotional uplift which makes no costly demands and which fails to distinguish between natural and Christian existence, then we cannot help treating the cross as an ordinary everyday calamity.... We have then forgotten that the cross means rejection and shame as well as suffering.... Only a man thus totally committed in discipleship can experience the meaning of the cross.

—Dietrich Bonhoeffer[78]

What does resurrection mean for us? It means forgetting the language of the oppressor; it means a change in lifestyle; and it means new community. All these experiences which people have when they get involved with the cross are simultaneously political and theological changes. The radicalization is not divisible. To become more devout works out in practice in society as becoming more radical. Political radicalization also means new spirituality. I think it is a catastrophic mistake if in the Christian tradition we bring about a division of labor between those who fight and those who pray, those who risk action designed to change the world and those who seek strength and renewal in prayer and reading the Bible. Struggle and contemplation belong together. A division of labor in this central self-expression of faith is deadly; it makes the people who fight blind and brutal, and the people who pray sentimental and deaf to the cries without. —Dorothee Sölle[79]

In the Gospels...what is specifically costly in following Christ comes from the praxis of announcing the good news of God, of building up the kingdom, and of confronting the anti-kingdom. In Mark's Gospel, right from the start Jesus became involved in serious conflicts precisely for acting on behalf of the kingdom. He healed in the synagogue on the Sabbath, and "the Pharisees went out and immediately held counsel with the Herodians against him, to see how to destroy him" (Mark 3:6). It was the beginning of a persecution that finally led to his crucifixion...because he was confronting the anti-kingdom head-on. —Jon Sobrino, S.J.[80]

EIGHT

New People of God

In his ministry, Jesus gathered together his disciples into a community and gave them a mission, sending them out into the world to work for the coming of the kingdom. These two dimensions, community and mission, have been at the root of the Christian community from the difficult moment before Pentecost, when they were hiding for fear of persecution, until today where the Holy Spirit continues to guide the church.

Unfortunately, as we know, throughout Christian history, the Christian community has not always lived up to its vocation. Christ's followers have become divided, church structures and leaders have occasionally been entangled with concerns for money and power, and the concerns for justice and the marginalized have been forgotten. As we can see in the Acts of the Apostles and the different epistles, these struggles are not new. The Christian community has long struggled with maintaining unity while being a prophetic agent in the world. In the midst of this, we have seen great witnesses, martyrs and saints who have helped us to continue on the correct path.

As part of this, Christian leaders have developed a rich corpus of social teaching, which helps us respond to the "signs of the times" (Matt. 16:1–3) from the faith perspective. Sadly, however, it seems that many Christians, especially those in economic or political power, have not fully understood these teachings.

- *How does the church today reflect its dual mission of community and prophetic action in the world?*
- *Does the church make clear to its members the social dimension of the faith?*

The Christian Community

They were faithful to the teaching of the apostles, the common life of sharing, the breaking of the bread and the prayers. ...Now all the believers lived together and shared all their belongings. They would sell their property and all they had and distribute the proceeds to others according to their need. Each day they met together in the Temple area; they broke bread in their homes; they shared their food with great joy and simplicity of heart; they praised God and won the people's favor. —Acts 2:42, 44–47

A church that does not join the poor, in order to speak out from the side of the poor against the injustices committed against them, is not the true church of Jesus Christ.

—Archbishop Oscar Romero[81]

Christians, if they are not doing so already, must quite simply participate in the struggle for liberation and for a just society.

—*Kairos Document*[82]

In a phase of world capitalism such as the one we are presently enduring, real and visible alternatives are more necessary than ever; simple, moralizing invocations of justice are not sufficient. Even people of a secular mind-set who are seeking alternatives to the dominant system concur in affirming the need to establish new economic forms from the grassroots. From a Christian perspective, this is precisely what faith makes possible. Christians can give the world the good news that another way of life is already possible, and is already at work in history.

—Antonio Gonzalez[83]

The attitude of the church to globalization has to be taken with inspiration from the teaching and life of Jesus Christ. The teaching of Jesus is diametrically opposed to the values and negative results of capitalistic globalization. An essential and indispensable aspect of Jesus' teaching is love and unselfish service to the poor, the oppressed, and marginalized.

—Tissa Balasuriya, O.M.I.[84]

Sons and Daughters of God

Now in Christ Jesus, all of you are sons and daughters of God through faith. All of you who were given to Christ through baptism have put on Christ. Here there is no longer any difference between Jew or Greek, or between slave or freed, or between man and woman: but all of you are one in Christ Jesus. —Galatians 3:26–28

The word "new" appears again and again to describe what God wants and what God does: a new song, a new heart, a new spirit, a new person, a new life, a new creature, a new covenant, new wine in new wineskins, a new heaven and a new earth, a new Jerusalem.

The truth of the matter is that the God of the Bible is a God of newness and change (see Isa. 43:18–19). What God stands for is a whole new world; it is God who wants to make all things new (Rev. 21:5)....The new Exodus or new heaven and new earth make no sense unless we recall the first Exodus and the old heaven and old earth. God was faithful in the past and will be lovingly faithful in the future. God was inventive in the past and God will prove even more lovingly inventive and innovative in the future.

The problem is that most of us do not want to change our personal lives. We can want many changes — political, social, economic, religious, or congregational — but we do not want to introduce anything new into our personal lives. The world, church, and congregation cannot change very much more until people begin to change. To go further into the kind of newness that God wants, each one of us must look more deeply into our own need for change.

Nothing blocks God's plan for a new world more effectively than complacent, self-righteous people who cannot see that something totally and radically new is needed in their personal lives and their attitudes to others. Yes, others do need to change, but you and I also need to change. —Barbara Davis, R.S.G.[85]

Christ Is Our Peace

At that time you were without Christ, you did not belong to the community of Israel; the covenant of God and his promises were not for you; you had no hope and were without God in this world. But now, in Christ Jesus and by his blood, you who were once far off have come near.

For Christ is our peace, he who has made the two peoples one, destroying in his one flesh the wall — the hatred — which separated us. He abolished the Law with its precepts. He made peace in

NEW PEOPLE OF GOD — 133

uniting the two peoples in him, creating out of the two one New Man. He destroyed hatred and reconciled us both to God through the cross, making two one body. He came to proclaim peace.
—Ephesians 2:12–17

Resurrection brings more than new clothes or Easter baskets. It means peace is stronger than war, justice stronger than injustice, compassion than contempt. We prove we're a resurrection people by putting down our swords and beating them into plowshares. By loving our enemies. By carrying on Jesus' work of nonviolent resistance against systemic injustice. By speaking out against the insane U.S. war on Iraq. And by persisting despite the obstacles, the opposition, and the apparent futility, knowing that the outcome, in God's hands, is assured.
—John Dear, S.J.[86]

It is not we who construct God's reign. Rather, we must receive it like the child who is surprised by an unexpected gift, not like the adult who boasts of his works.... This does not exclude one's own effort. Quite the contrary; in a capitalist world dominated by the logic of self-justification, our work is more necessary than ever. It will be an effective work, however, only when we understand clearly and proclaim plainly that the reign belongs to God, and that it is God himself who has initiated it in history through the Messiah. —Antonio Gonzalez[87]

You Are One Body

As the body is one, having many members, and all the members, while being many, form one body, so it is with Christ. All of us, whether Jews or Greeks, slaves or free, have been baptized in one Spirit to

form one body, and all of us have been given to drink from the one Spirit. . . . God himself arranged the body in this way, giving more honor to those parts of the body that need it, so that the body may not be divided, but rather each member may care for the others. When one suffers, all of them suffer, and when one receives honor, all rejoice together.
—1 Corinthians 12:12–13, 25–26

The solidarity which binds all men together as members of a common family makes it impossible for wealthy nations to look with indifference upon the hunger, misery, and poverty of other nations whose citizens are unable to enjoy even elementary human rights. The nations of the world are becoming more and more dependent on one another, and it will not be possible to preserve a lasting peace so long as glaring economic and social imbalances persist. —Pope John XXIII[88]

In God himself, believers would find the model of what God desires to create in history: a loving community of free and equal persons. Nonetheless, it is not altogether clear that this linking of the kingdom of God and the Trinity is truly liberating. —Antonio Gonzalez[89]

Community is like a large mosaic. Each little piece seems so insignificant. One piece is bright red, another cold blue or dull green, another warm purple, another sharp yellow, another shining gold. Some look precious, others ordinary. Some look valuable, others worthless. Some look gaudy, others delicate. As individual stones, we can do little with them except compare them and judge their beauty and value. When, however, all these little stones are brought together in one big mosaic portraying the face of Christ, who would ever question the importance of any one of them? If one of them, even the least spectacular one, is missing, the face is incomplete. Together in the one mosaic, each little stone is indispensable and makes a unique contribution to the glory of God. That's community, a fellowship of little people who together make God visible in the world. —Henri Nouwen[90]

He Emptied Himself

If we share the same spirit and are capable of mercy and compassion, then I beg of you make me very happy: have one love, one spirit, one feeling, do nothing through rivalry or vain conceit. On the contrary let each of you gently consider the others as more important than yourselves. Do not seek your own interest, but rather

that of others. Your attitude should be the same as Jesus Christ had: Though he was in the form of God he did not regard equality with God as something to be grasped, but emptied himself, taking on the nature of a servant, made in human likeness, and in his appearance found as a man. He humbled himself by being obedient to death, death on the cross.
—Philippians 2:2–11

We are called to make concrete and visible the signs of our repentance and to offer them in all humility to the ones who have suffered from our unjust ways. We are called to risk all in the cosmic effort to live justly. We are called to shape our journeys in a manner explicitly informed by the Gospel we proclaim. We are called to resist evil, but to go beyond resistance into life "as if," and to believe that in the process of profound conversion we will discover who we are, who are our brothers and sisters, how we are to live with all of creation, and toward what vision of life we are to journey together. —Marie Dennis[91]

New Life

By this baptism in his death, we were buried with Christ and, as Christ was raised from among the dead by the glory of the Father, so we begin walking in a new life.

So you, too, must consider yourselves dead to sin and alive to God in Christ Jesus. Do not allow sin any control over your mortal bodies; do not submit yourselves to its evil inclinations, and do not give your members over to sin, as instruments to do evil. On the contrary, offer yourselves as persons returned from death to life, and let the members of your body be as holy instruments at the service of God. —Romans 6:4, 11–13

In the Catholic Tradition, responsible citizenship is a virtue, and participation in political life is a moral obligation. This obligation is rooted in our baptismal commitment to follow Jesus Christ and to bear Christian witness in all we do. —U.S. Catholic Bishops[92]

Peacemaking is not an optional commitment. It is a requirement of our faith. We are called to be peacemakers, not by some movement of the moment, but by our Lord Jesus. The content and context of our peacemaking is set not by some political agenda or ideological program, but by the teaching of his church.

—Maryann Cusimano Love[93]

The reign of God...is not a utopia for the future, but a dynamism that is already acting in history. The reign is already present there where Jesus reigns, in the community of his disciples. This community, however, is not the reign of God.... This Spirit, although it blows where it will, becomes explicitly present there where believers can call God "Father" without fear, forming fraternal communities of brothers and sisters.... It is in the Christian communities, however, that the most subversive and radical transformation begins to occur, because in them the power of Adam's sin has disappeared and, with it, all the consequent forms of dependency, oppression and death. —Antonio Gonzalez[94]

Do Not Be Conformed

Don't let yourselves be shaped by the world where you live, but rather be transformed through the renewal of your mind. You must discern the will of God: what is good, what pleases, what is perfect.
—Romans 12:2

Every action of ours must be accompanied by a reflection to orient it, to order it, to make it coherent, so that it does not lapse into a sterile and superficial activism. —Gustavo Gutiérrez[95]

The first task of a prophetic theology for our times would be an attempt at social analysis or what Jesus would call "reading the signs of the times" (Matt. 16:3). —*Kairos Document*[96]

NEW PEOPLE OF GOD — 143

To whom do we belong? This is really a question of worship, of baptism, and of fundamental Christian identity. It's a critical question, because other identities—competing senses of belonging—are always tugging at Christians.... Because the Body of Christ is an international community, we are called to be Christians first and members of our tribes or nations second.... Support for U.S. wars and foreign policy is still the area where American Christians are most "conformed to the world" (Rom. 12:2). This is our Achilles' heel, our biggest blind spot, our least questioned allegiance, the worst compromise of our Christian identity, and the greatest failing of our Christian obedience. —Jim Wallis[97]

Love

See what singular love the Father has for us: we are called children of God, and we really are... we love our brothers and sisters, and with this we know that we have passed from death to life. The one who does not love remains in death.

The one who hates his brother is a murderer, and, as you know, eternal life does not remain in the murderer.

This is how we have known what love is: he gave his life for us. We, too, ought to give our life for our brothers and sisters. If anyone enjoys the riches of this world, but closes his heart when he sees his brother or sister in need, how will the love of God remain in him? My dear children, let us love not only with words and with our lips, but in truth and in deed.   —1 John 3:1, 14–18

God and love are inseparable. It is not possible — and this is probably the gravest error of all conservative theologies — to tear God and love apart and to say that God is primary and permanent while love is some secondary, derivative thing. The Gospel never tells us to believe first, then love. It describes the achievement of Christian life in terms of unity: In loving, we believe. In loving, we depend on something other than ourselves.

—Dorothee Sölle[98]

Those who think love or charity is in opposition to justice are flat wrong. If all we are about is politics or trying to change structures, we run the real risk of becoming love-less manipulators. If all we think about is individual personal charity or love, then we leave unjust institutions and structures in place that constantly dehumanize, oppress, and wound our sisters and brothers. We need both in our societies and in our lives. This call to love tenderly is personal but not only personal. We all know we must love our neighbor, but social justice pushes us to constantly expand the definition of neighbor. —Bill Quigley[99]

NINE

A New Creation

Scripture calls the Christian community to hope in the coming of God's kingdom, a new way of being where suffering and injustice will be no more. This is not just an idealistic vision of something to happen on a different spiritual plane of existence, but it is something that we believe will happen in history.

Followers and disciples of Jesus Christ are not only called to hope in this future way, but also to work, with God's help, toward that end. As such, Christians cannot separate faith from everyday life. What Christians do on Sunday cannot be separated from what is done on Monday.

- *What obstacles are there for us to live an integral faith?*

Behold I Make All Things New

Then I saw a new heaven and a new earth. The first heaven and the first earth had passed away and no longer was there any sea. I saw the new Jerusalem, the holy city coming down from God.... A loud voice came from the throne, "Here is the dwelling of God among mortals: he will pitch his tent among them and they will be his people; he will be God-with-them.

He will wipe every tear from their eyes. There shall be no more death or mourning, crying out or pain, for the world that was has passed away." The

A NEW CREATION

One seated on the throne said, "See I make all things new." —Revelation 21:1–5

I could not be leading a religious life unless I identified myself with the whole of humanity, and that I could not do unless I took part in politics. The whole gamut of humanity's activities constitutes an indivisible whole. You cannot divide social, economic, political, and purely religious work into watertight compartments. I do not know of any religion apart from human activity. It provides a moral basis to all other activities which they would otherwise lack. —Mohandas Gandhi[100]

Some want to keep a Gospel so disembodied that it does not get involved at all in the world it must save. Christ is now in history. Christ is in the womb of the people. Christ is now bringing about a new heaven and a new earth.

—Archbishop Oscar Romero[101]

Statistics often paint a bleak picture of reality. Sometimes this is necessary. But statistics don't show the full picture. They don't reveal the resilience of the human spirit. They don't reveal that in the midst of such suffering, there is hope. This is important, because the sheer immensity of the problem of global poverty can be overwhelming. We have to overcome that feeling of helplessness, the feeling that there is nothing that can be done....

Global poverty is not a fact of life. It can — and must — be eradicated. The international community cannot ignore this issue.... Shortly before my visit to Portugal last year, another startling image appeared in the media. The picture showed a huge fishing net being towed behind a trawler. But on closer inspection, it revealed a chilling reality: around the edge of the net, twenty-seven migrants were clinging on for their lives. They had been abandoned by people traffickers in a small wooden boat that soon began to sink. The captain of the trawler refused to take them on board, fearing that a change in course would jeopardize his valuable catch of tuna. So they clung to the net, ignored by the captain, until rescued by the Italian navy.

It was a powerful metaphor for our world: the poorest people clinging precariously to life, as we steam blindly on in pursuit of greater wealth. We need to stop this ship. And we need to get the world's poor on board now. And then together, as one humanity, we need to set a new course for a better future.

—Lesley-Anne Knight[102]

Suggestions for Action

The following is a brief resource list of some of the many organizations, movements, and networks concerned with the Gospel call to peace and justice:

Media Resources

America Magazine
www.americamagazine.org

Catholic Worker Movement/
Dorothy Day Library
www.catholicworker.org

Commonweal
www.commonwealmagazine.org

Cristianisme i Justícia Study Center
www.fespinal.com

Writings and reflections of
Fr. John Dear, S.J.
www.fatherjohndear.org

National Catholic Reporter
www.ncronline.org

Orbis Books
www.orbisbooks.com

Sojourners: Christians for Justice and Peace
www.sojo.net

American Peace and Justice Networks

Catholics in Alliance for the Common Good
www.catholicsinalliance.org

Catholic Relief Services
www.crs.org

SUGGESTIONS FOR ACTION — 155

Catholics United
www.catholics-united.org

Center of Concern
www.coc.org

Christian Peacemaker Teams
www.cpt.org

Fellowship of Reconciliation
www.forusa.org

Maryknoll Office for Global Concerns
www.maryknollogc.org

National Catholic Student Coalition
www.catholicstudent.org

Network Social Justice Lobby
www.networklobby.org

Pax Christi USA
www.paxchristiusa.org

Voices in the Wilderness
www.vitw.org

Global Peace and Justice Networks

Caritas Internationalis
www.caritas.org

Franciscans International
www.franciscansinternational.org

Pax Christi International
www.paxchristi.net

Pax Romana-ICMICA (Catholic professionals and intellectuals)
www.icmica-miic.org

World Council of Churches
www.wcc-coe.org

World Conference of Religions for Peace
www.wcrp.org

SUGGESTIONS FOR ACTION

Global Youth Networks and Movements

International Movement of Catholic Agricultural and Rural Youth (MIJARC)
   www.mijarc.org

International Movement of Catholic Students (IMCS-Pax Romana)
   www.imcs-miec.org

International Coordination of Young Christian Workers (CIJOC)
   www.cijoc.org

International Young Christian Workers (JOCI)
   www.jociycw.net

World Alliance of YMCAs
   www.ymca.int

World Council of Churches Youth Desk
  www.ecumenicalyouth.org

World Student Christian Federation (WSCF)
  www.wscfglobal.org

World Young Women's Christian Association (YWCA)
  www.worldywca.org

Further Reading

Modern Spiritual Masters Series from Orbis Books

Dietrich Bonhoeffer (edited by Robert Coles)

Henri Nouwen (edited by Robert A. Jonas)

Oscar Romero (by Marie Dennis, Rennie Golden, and Scott Wright)

Thomas Merton (edited by Christine M. Bochen)

Thich Nhat Hanh (edited by Robert Ellsberg)

Mother Teresa (edited by Jean Maalouf)

Mohandas Gandhi (edited by John Dear)

Karl Rahner (edited by Philip Endean)

Dorothee Sölle (edited by Dianne L. Oliver)

Howard Thurman (edited by Luther E. Smith, Jr.)

Other Books

Bernardin, Joseph. *The Seamless Garment: Writings on the Consistent Ethic of Life.* Ed. Thomas A. Nairn. Maryknoll, N.Y.: Orbis Books, 2008.

Between Honesty and Hope; Documents From and About the Church in Latin America. Issued at Lima by the Peruvian Bishops' Commission for Social Action. Maryknoll, N.Y.: Maryknoll Publications, 1970

Dennis, Marie. *A Diversity of Vocations.* Maryknoll, N.Y.: Orbis Books, 2008.

Gonzalez, Antonio. *The Gospel of Faith and Justice.* Maryknoll, N.Y.: Orbis Books, 2005.

Gutiérrez, Gustavo. *Gustavo Gutiérrez: Essential Writings.* Ed. James B. Nickoloff. Maryknoll, N.Y.: Orbis Books, 1997.

FURTHER READING

Nolan, Albert. *Jesus Today: A Spirituality of Radical Freedom.* Maryknoll, N.Y.: Orbis Books, 2006.

Sobrino, Jon. *No Salvation outside the Poor: Prophetic-Utopian Essays.* Maryknoll, N.Y.: Orbis Books, 2008.

Tutu, Desmond. *No Future without Forgiveness.* New York: Image Books, 1999.

Notes

1. UN *Human Development Report* (2005), 3.
2. UN *Human Development Report* (2007/2008), *www.undp.org*, and the Coalition of Catholic Organizations Against Human Trafficking, *www.usccb.org*.
3. Catholic Campaign for Human Development, *www.usccb.org/cchd/povertyusa*, and see also the U.S. Department of Defense, *www.defenselink.mil*.
4. *Kairos Document*, issued by South African theologians and church leaders (1985).
5. Thich Nhat Hanh, Vietnamese Zen Buddhist monk and peace leader, *The Sun My Heart: From Mindfulness to Insight Contemplation* (Berkeley, Calif.: Parallax Press, 1988).

6. Pope John Paul II, 1999 World Day of Peace Message, *Respect for Human Rights: The Secret of True Peace*, 4.

7. Cardinal Joseph Bernardin, former Catholic archbishop of Chicago, *The Seamless Garment, Writings on the Consistent Ethic of Life*, 16–17.

8. U.S. Catholic Bishops, *Forming Conscience for Faithful Citizenship* (2007), 87.

9. UN *Human Development Report* (2007/2008), 2.

10. Pope Benedict XVI, World Day of Peace Message (2007), *The Human Person, the Heart of Peace*, 8.

11. *Charter of Catholic Student Rights and Responsibilities*, issued by the International Movement of Catholic Students and the International Young Catholic Students (2007).

12. Archbishop Desmond Tutu, retired Anglican archbishop of Capetown, South Africa, *No Future without Forgiveness*, 31.

13. Preamble of the *Earth Charter*.

14. *Kairos Document,* issued by South African theologians and church leaders (1985).

15. Letter of the Peoples of the Third World, signed by eighteen Third World Catholic bishops, in *Between Honesty and Hope,* 10.

16. Howard Thurman, Protestant minister and civil rights activist, *The Luminous Darkness* (New York: Harper & Row, 1965; Richmond, Ind.: Friends United Press, 1989).

17. Pope John Paul II, encyclical letter *Sollicitudo Rei Socialis* (1987), 38.

18. Cardinal Joseph Bernardin, former Catholic archbishop of Chicago, *The Seamless Garment, Writings on the Consistent Ethic of Life,* 295.

19. Pontifical Council for Justice and Peace, *Compendium of the Social Doctrine of the Church,* 297–98.

20. Jon Sobrino, S.J., *No Salvation outside the Poor,* 37–38.

21. U.S. Catholic Bishops, *Forming Conscience for Faithful Citizenship* (2007), 83.

22. Catholic Bishops of Kenya, *On the Burden of International Debt* (2005), 4, 8.

23. World Council of Churches, *Lead Us Not into Temptation: Churches' Response to the Policies of the International Financial Institutions, a Background Document* (2001), 22–23.

24. Albert Nolan, O.P., South African theologian, *Jesus Today: A Spirituality of Radical Freedom*, 15–16.

25. Muhammad Yunus, founder of Grameen Bank, Bangladesh, Nobel Peace Prize Acceptance Speech (2006).

26. Antonio Gonzalez, *The Gospel of Faith and Justice*, 12.

27. Dr. Martin Luther King, Jr., Nobel Peace Prize Acceptance Speech (1964).

28. UN *Human Development Report* (2007/2008), 2.

29. Oscar Romero, martyred Catholic Archbishop of San Salvador, *Monseñor Oscar A. Romero: Su pensamiento*, vol. 5, November 26, 1978, homily, 327.

30. Mohandas Gandhi, *The Collected Works of Mahatma Gandhi,* vol. 33, March 31, 1927 (Ahmedabad: Navajivan Pub., 1967–84).

31. Oscar Romero, *A Shepherd's Diary,* trans. Irene Hodgson (Cincinnati: St. Anthony Messenger Press, 1996).

32. Albert Nolan, O.P., *Jesus Today: A Spirituality of Radical Freedom,* 31.

33. Kofi Annan, former United Nations Secretary General, Nobel Peace Prize Acceptance Speech (2001).

34. Helene O'Sullivan, M.M., Maryknoll Sister, "Stopping Traffic" in *Maryknoll* magazine (November 2003).

35. Thomas Merton, Trappist monk and spiritual writer, *Faith and Violence* (Notre Dame, Ind.: University of Notre Dame Press, 1968).

36. Second Vatican Council, *Gaudium et Spes,* 66.

37. Kathy Kelly, American peace leader, "Being Hope" (May 31, 2007), at Voices for

Creative Nonviolence, *http://vcnv.org/being-hope*.

38. Dom Helder Camara, former archbishop of Olinda and Recife, Brazil, in *LADOC*, 1:30.

39. Gustavo Gutiérrez, Peruvian theologian, presentation at a meeting of the National Office for Social Research in Chimbote, Peru (July 1968).

40. Bill Quigley, social justice lawyer, "Social Justice Spirituality: A Meditation on Micah 6:8," in *Blueprint for Social Justice* 58, no. 1 (September 2004): 1–2.

41. Dietrich Bonhoeffer, German Lutheran theologian, "Jesus Christ and the Essence of Christianity," address delivered in Barcelona on December 11, 1928. Translation reprinted from Geffrey B. Kelly and F. Burton Nelson, eds., *A Testament to Freedom: The Essential Writings of Dietrich Bonhoeffer* (New York: HarperCollins, 1990).

42. Mother Teresa, founder of the Missionaries of Charity, *In My Own Words*,

comp. José Luis González-Balado (Liguori, Mo.: Liguori Publications, 1996).

43. Thomas Merton, *No Man Is an Island* (New York: Harcourt Brace, 1955).

44. John Dear, S.J., Jesuit peace leader, "On Moral Leadership: The Need for Prophets for Peace and Justice in a Culture of War and Injustice" (October 2005), at *www.fatherjohndear.org*.

45. UN *Human Development Report* (2007/2008), 2.

46. U.S. Catholic Bishops, *Forming Conscience for Faithful Citizenship* (2007), 88.

47. Wangari Maathai, founder of the Greenbelt Movement, Kenya, Nobel Peace Prize Acceptance Speech (2004).

48. Thomas Merton, *New Seeds of Contemplation* (New York: New Directions, 1962).

49. Frida Berrigan, American Catholic peace leader, *Sojourners* (June 2008).

50. Jim Wallis, evangelical social leader, "A Call to Repentance," *Sojourners* (January 2008), 12–17.

51. Thich Nhat Hanh, *Going Home: Jesus and Buddha as Brothers* (New York: Riverhead Books, 1999).

52. John Dear, S.J., "Mary of Nazareth, Prophet of Nonviolence" (December 2001), at *www.fatherjohndear.org*.

53. Marie Dennis, co-president of Pax Christi International and director of the Maryknoll Office for Global Concerns, *A Diversity of Vocations*, 111.

54. Gustavo Gutiérrez, presentation at a meeting of the National Office for Social Research in Chimbote, Peru (July 1968).

55. U.S. Catholic Bishops, *Economic Justice for All* (1986), 16.

56. Musimbi Kanyoro, general secretary of the World Young Women's Christian Association, presentation to the 2005 World Forum on Theology and Liberation.

57. Marie Dennis, *A Diversity of Vocations*, 94.

58. Dorothy Day, co-founder of the Catholic Worker Movement, "On Pilgrimage — December 1972," *Catholic Worker*

(December 1972), 2, 8, at the Dorothy Day Library, *www.catholicworker.org*.

59. Marie Nassaur, M.M., Maryknoll Sister, "A Friend on Death Row" in *Maryknoll* magazine (July–August 2003).

60. Oscar Romero, *Monseñor Oscar A. Romero: Su pensamiento,* vols. 1–2, April 7, 1977, homily, 14.

61. Mother Teresa, *A Gift for God: Prayers and Meditations* (New York: Harper & Row, 1975).

62. Jon Sobrino, S.J., *No Salvation outside the Poor,* 25.

63. Catholic Bishops of Kenya, *On the Burden of International Debt* (2005), 5.

64. Oscar Romero, *The Violence of Love,* comp. and trans. James R. Brockman (Farmington, Pa.: Plough Publishing House, 1998; Maryknoll, N.Y.: Orbis Books, 2004).

65. Adela Cortina and Ignasi Carreras, "I Buy...Therefore I Am..." in *Cristianisme i Justícia,* no. 116 (2003): 12.

66. Karl Rahner, S.J., German Jesuit theologian, *Sehnsucht nach dem geheimnisvollen Gott*.

67. Tissa Balasuriya, O.M.I., Sri Lankan theologian, "Challenges of Globalization to the Universal Church," talk given at the World Social Forum in Mumbai, India (2004).

68. Marie Dennis, *A Diversity of Vocations*, 96.

69. UNICEF, *Progress of Nations* (2000).

70. Dorothy Day, "Love Is the Measure," in *Catholic Worker* (June 1946), 2, at the Dorothy Day Library, *www.catholicworker.org*.

71. Thomas Merton, *Love and Living*, ed. Naomi Burton Stone and Brother Patrick Hart (New York: Farrar, Straus & Giroux, 1979).

72. Lush Gjergji, *Mother Teresa: To Live, to Love, to Witness — Her Spiritual Way*, trans. Jordan Aumann, O.P. (Hyde Park, N.Y.: New City Press, 1995).

73. Mohandas Gandhi, *The Collected Works of Mahatma Gandhi*, vol. 83, April 6, 1946 (Ahmedabad: Navajivan Pub., 1967–84).

74. John Dear, S.J., "The Eucharist and Nonviolence: Remembering, Reconciling, and Sending Us Forth to Make Peace," at *www.fatherjohndear.org*.

75. Navin Chawla, *Mother Teresa: The Authorized Biography* (Boston: Element, 1992).

76. Robert Bellah, "Flaws in the Protestant Code" in *Ethical Perspectives* 7, no. 4 (2000): 298.

77. Blessed Pier Giorgio Frassati, Italian Catholic student leader.

78. Dietrich Bonhoeffer, *The Cost of Discipleship*, trans. R. H. Fuller with revisions by Irmgard Booth (New York: Macmillan, 1963).

79. Dorothee Sölle, German theologian, *Choosing Life*, trans. Margaret Kohl from *Wählt das Leben*, 1980 (Philadelphia: Fortress Press, 1981).

80. Jon Sobrino, S.J., *No Salvation outside the Poor*, 93.

81. Oscar Romero, *The Violence of Love*.

82. *Kairos Document,* issued by South African theologians and church leaders (1985).

83. Antonio Gonzalez, *The Gospel of Faith and Justice,* 39.

84. Tissa Balasuriya, O.M.I., "Challenges of Globalization to the Universal Church," talk given at the World Social Forum in Mumbai, India (2004).

85. Barbara Davis, R.S.G., Australian Good Shepherd Sister, in *We Are Caught into This Mystery: Excerpts From the Writings and Reflections of Barbara Davis, R.S.G.*

86. John Dear, S.J., "Resurrection!" (April 2007), at *www.fatherjohndear.org.*

87. Antonio Gonzalez, *The Gospel of Faith and Justice,* 91.

88. Pope John XXIII, encyclical letter *Mater et Magistra* (1961), 157.

89. Antonio Gonzalez, *The Gospel of Faith and Justice,* 147.

90. Henri Nouwen, Dutch Catholic priest and spiritual writer, *Can You Drink the Cup?* (Notre Dame, Ind.: Ave Maria Press, 1996).

91. Marie Dennis, *A Diversity of Vocations*, 45.

92. U.S. Catholic Bishops, *Forming Conscience for Faithful Citizenship* (2007), 13.

93. Maryann Cusimano Love, "Building Peace" in *America* magazine (March 31, 2008).

94. Antonio Gonzalez, *The Gospel of Faith and Justice*, 157.

95. Gustavo Gutiérrez, presentation at a meeting of the National Office for Social Research in Chimbote, Peru (July 1968).

96. *Kairos Document,* issued by South African theologians and church leaders (1985).

97. Jim Wallis, "A Call to Repentance," in *Sojourners* (January 2008): 12–17.

98. Dorothee Sölle, *The Strength of the Weak: Toward a Christian Feminist Identity,* trans. Robert and Rita Kimber (Philadelphia: Westminster Press, 1984).

99. Bill Quigley, "Social Justice Spirituality: A Meditation on Micah 6:8" in *Blueprint*

for Social Justice 58, no. 1 (September 2004): 3.

100. Mohandas Gandhi, *The Collected Works of Mahatma Gandhi*, vol. 62, December 24, 1935 (Ahmedabad: Navajivan Pub., 1967–84).

101. Oscar Romero, *The Violence of Love*.

102. Lesley-Anne Knight, secretary general, Caritas Internationalis, "Campaigning against Global Poverty," plenary speech to the 2008 U.S. Catholic Social Ministry Gathering (February 25, 2008).